Data Protection 101

Neil King

Table Of Contents

Data Protection 101: A Beginner's Guide to Digital Security

Data Protection 101: A Beginner's Guide to Digital Security

Chapter 1: Introduction to Data Protection

What is Data Protection?

In today's digital age, data protection has become a critical concern for businesses and individuals alike. With the increasing amount of data being generated and shared online, the need for effective data protection measures has never been greater. But what exactly is data protection, and why is it so important?

At its core, data protection refers to the measures that are taken to safeguard sensitive information from unauthorized access, use, or disclosure. This can include a wide range of different types of data, such as personal information, financial data, intellectual property, and more. Data protection can be achieved through a variety of different methods, including encryption, access controls, backups, and more.

One of the primary reasons why data protection is so important is because of the potential consequences of a data breach. If sensitive information falls into the wrong hands, it can be used for a variety of nefarious purposes, such as identity theft, fraud, or cyber attacks. In addition, businesses that suffer a data breach can face significant financial and reputational damage, as well as legal liability.

Another important aspect of data protection is data privacy. This refers to the right of individuals to control their own personal information, and to have it protected from unauthorized access or use. With the increasing amount of data being generated and shared online, it is more important than ever to ensure that individuals' privacy rights are respected and protected.

Overall, data protection is a critical concern for anyone who generates, stores, or shares sensitive information online. Whether you are a business owner, an individual consumer, or a cybersecurity professional, it is important to understand the importance of data protection and to take steps to ensure that your data is safeguarded from unauthorized access or use. By implementing effective data protection measures, you can help to protect yourself, your business, and your customers from the potentially devastating consequences of a data breach.

Why is Data Protection Important?

In today's digital age, data is an essential asset of any business. From customer information to financial records, data holds the key to a company's success. However, with the rise of cyber attacks, data protection has become a crucial aspect of business and organizational operations.

Data protection refers to the practice of safeguarding sensitive information from unauthorized access, use, or disclosure. The importance of data protection cannot be overstated, as it helps to ensure the privacy, safety, and security of personal and sensitive information. Here are a few reasons why data protection is essential:

1. Compliance with regulations: In recent years, governments around the world have introduced strict data protection regulations such as the GDPR and CCPA. Organizations that fail to comply with these regulations face severe penalties and reputational damage.

2. Protecting customer trust: Consumers are becoming increasingly aware of the importance of data protection. A data breach can damage a company's reputation and erode consumer trust, leading to a loss of business.

3. Preventing financial loss: Data breaches can be expensive, with costs ranging from legal fees and fines to lost revenue and damage to brand reputation.

4. Ensuring business continuity: A cyber attack can disrupt business operations, leading to downtime and financial losses. Data protection measures can help minimize the impact of a cyber attack and ensure business continuity.

5. Mitigating cyber threats: Cyber threats are constantly evolving, and organizations must take proactive measures to protect their sensitive information. Data protection measures such as encryption, access controls, and regular backups can help mitigate the risk of cyber attacks.

In conclusion, data protection is critical for any business or organization that deals with sensitive information. By implementing data protection measures, organizations can ensure compliance with regulations, protect customer trust, prevent financial loss, ensure business continuity, and mitigate cyber threats.

Who Needs Data Protection?

In today's digital age, data protection is no longer an option but a necessity. Every individual and organization that uses technology to store, process, or transmit data needs data protection. The consequences of failing to protect data can be catastrophic and far-reaching, not just for the organization but for its employees, customers, and partners.

Cybersecurity professionals and network administrators are responsible for ensuring the security of their organization's data. They need to stay up-to-date with the latest threats and vulnerabilities, and implement appropriate security measures to prevent unauthorized access, theft, or damage to data. Cloud security has become a critical area of concern, as more and more organizations move their data to the cloud. Cloud service providers must ensure that their infrastructure and applications are secure and compliant with data protection regulations.

Mobile device security is another essential aspect of data protection. Mobile devices, including smartphones and tablets, are now an integral part of our daily lives. They store a vast amount of personal and sensitive data, including emails, contacts, messages, and financial information. Mobile device security should encompass both physical and digital security measures, such as passcodes, biometric authentication, encryption, and remote wipe capabilities.

Data privacy and protection are crucial for any organization that collects, processes, or stores personal data. Data protection regulations, such as the General Data Protection Regulation (GDPR) and the California Consumer Privacy Act (CCPA), require organizations to implement appropriate technical and organizational measures to protect personal data from unauthorized access, use, or disclosure. Failure to comply with these regulations can result in hefty fines and damage to the organization's reputation.

Finally, cyber threat intelligence is essential for identifying and mitigating cyber threats. Cyber threat intelligence refers to the collection, analysis, and dissemination of information about potential cyber threats. It helps organizations stay ahead of cybercriminals and prevent cyber attacks before they occur.

In conclusion, anyone who uses technology to store, process, or transmit data needs data protection. Cybersecurity, network security, cloud security, mobile device security, data privacy and protection, and cyber threat intelligence are all critical areas of concern for organizations that want to protect their data and stay ahead of cyber threats. By implementing appropriate security measures and staying up-to-date with the latest threats and vulnerabilities, organizations can ensure the safety and integrity of their data.

Chapter 2: Cybersecurity

What is Cybersecurity?

What is Cybersecurity?

Cybersecurity refers to the practice of protecting computers, networks, servers, mobile devices, and other connected devices from unauthorized access, theft, damage, or disruption. It involves a range of technologies, processes, and policies designed to safeguard digital information and systems from cyber threats such as hacking, malware, phishing, identity theft, ransomware, and other forms of cybercrime.

The need for cybersecurity has become increasingly important as more and more businesses and individuals rely on digital technology to store and transmit sensitive data. In recent years, cyber attacks have become more frequent, sophisticated, and costly, posing a significant threat to organizations of all sizes across industries, including healthcare, finance, retail, government, and more.

Effective cybersecurity involves a combination of technical and non-technical measures, including:

1) Network Security: This involves protecting the network infrastructure from unauthorized access, intrusion, and attacks. Common network security measures include firewalls, intrusion detection and prevention systems (IDS/IPS), virtual private networks (VPNs), and anti-virus software.

2) Cloud Security: This refers to securing data and applications stored in cloud-based environments such as public, private, and hybrid clouds. Cloud security measures include access controls, encryption, and data backup and recovery.

3) Mobile Device Security: This involves securing mobile devices such as smartphones, tablets, and laptops from cyber threats. Mobile device security measures include password protection, device encryption, and remote wipe capabilities.

4) Data Privacy and Protection: This refers to protecting sensitive information from unauthorized access, use, or disclosure. Data privacy and protection measures include data classification, access controls, encryption, and data backup and recovery.

Data Protection 101: A Beginner's Guide to Digital Security

5) Cyber Threat Intelligence: This involves gathering and analyzing information about potential cyber threats to identify and prevent attacks before they occur. Cyber threat intelligence measures include threat detection and analysis, vulnerability assessments, and risk management.

In conclusion, cybersecurity is a critical component of any organization's digital security strategy. By implementing comprehensive security measures, businesses can protect their data and systems from cyber threats and ensure the integrity and confidentiality of their sensitive information.

Types of Cybersecurity Threats

Types of Cybersecurity Threats

In today's digital age, cybersecurity threats pose a significant risk to businesses and individuals alike. The increasing sophistication and frequency of cyber-attacks have made it essential for organizations to have a comprehensive understanding of the different types of cybersecurity threats they may face. Here are some of the most common types of cybersecurity threats:

1. Malware: Malware is a malicious software that is designed to damage, disrupt, or gain unauthorized access to a computer system. This can include viruses, worms, trojans, and ransomware. Malware is often spread through email attachments, infected websites, and software downloads.

2. Phishing: Phishing is a fraudulent attempt to obtain sensitive information such as usernames, passwords, and credit card details. This is typically done through email, social media, or text messages that appear to be from a legitimate source. Phishing attacks can be highly effective because they often rely on social engineering tactics that trick the victim into divulging sensitive information.

3. Denial of Service (DoS) Attacks: A DoS attack is an attempt to make a website or network unavailable to users by overwhelming it with traffic. This can be done through the use of botnets, which are networks of infected computers that are controlled by a hacker.

4. Advanced Persistent Threats (APTs): APTs are sophisticated cyber-attacks that are specifically targeted at a particular organization or individual. These attacks often involve a combination of malware, social engineering, and other tactics to gain access to sensitive information.

5. Insider Threats: Insider threats refer to the risk posed by employees or contractors who have access to sensitive information. These individuals may intentionally or unintentionally cause harm to the organization by stealing data, installing malware, or simply being careless with sensitive information.

6. Internet of Things (IoT) Threats: As more devices become connected to the internet, the risk of cyber-attacks on these devices increases. IoT devices such as smart home appliances, medical devices, and industrial control systems can be vulnerable to attacks that could cause physical harm or disrupt critical systems.

In conclusion, cybersecurity threats are becoming increasingly sophisticated and diverse. To protect against these threats, businesses and individuals must stay informed of the latest threats and ensure they have the appropriate security measures in place. This includes regular software updates, employee training, and the use of security tools such as firewalls and antivirus software. By taking these steps, organizations can minimize their risk of falling victim to a cyber-attack and protect their sensitive information.

Cybersecurity Best Practices

Cybersecurity Best Practices

In the digital age, cybersecurity has become one of the most pressing issues for businesses of all sizes. The rise of cybercrime and the increasing sophistication of hackers and cybercriminals means that companies must take proactive measures to protect their data and systems from attack. In this subchapter, we will explore some of the best practices for cybersecurity that businesses can implement to safeguard their digital assets.

Network Security

Network security is the practice of protecting computer networks from unauthorized access or attack. One of the most effective ways to secure a network is to use robust passwords for all systems and devices. Strong passwords should be at least 12 characters long, include a mix of uppercase and lowercase letters, numbers, and special characters, and should be changed regularly.

Another crucial aspect of network security is to keep all software up to date. This includes operating systems, applications, and security software. Outdated software can have vulnerabilities that can be exploited by cybercriminals.

Cloud Security

Cloud computing has become a popular choice for businesses looking to store and access their data remotely. However, it also presents new security challenges. To ensure the security of cloud-based systems, businesses should use strong passwords and multi-factor authentication. They should also limit access to data to only those who need it and encrypt all sensitive data in transit and at rest.

Mobile Device Security

Mobile devices, such as smartphones and tablets, are increasingly used for work-related tasks. However, they can also be a weak point in a company's cybersecurity defenses. To secure mobile devices, businesses should use strong passwords and encryption, keep all software up to date, and use mobile device management (MDM) software to remotely wipe data from lost or stolen devices.

Data Privacy and Protection

Data privacy and protection are essential for businesses that store and process sensitive data. To ensure data privacy, businesses should limit access to data to only those who need it, encrypt all sensitive data in transit and at rest, and implement access control policies that restrict data access based on user roles.

Cyber Threat Intelligence

Cyber threat intelligence is the practice of monitoring and analyzing cyber threats to identify potential attacks and take proactive measures to prevent them. To implement cyber threat intelligence, businesses should use advanced threat detection and analysis tools, monitor social media and the dark web for potential threats, and share threat information with other organizations to improve overall cybersecurity defenses.

In conclusion, implementing these cybersecurity best practices can help businesses protect their digital assets from cyber threats. By using strong passwords, keeping software up to date, encrypting sensitive data, and implementing access controls and cyber threat intelligence, businesses can safeguard their networks, cloud-based systems, mobile devices, and data privacy and protection.

Cybersecurity Tools and Technologies

In today's digital age, cybersecurity has become a critical issue for businesses and individuals alike. With the rise of cyber attacks, it's crucial to understand the tools and technologies that can help protect your data and systems.

One of the most important cybersecurity tools is a firewall. Firewalls act as a barrier between your network and the internet, blocking unauthorized access and preventing malware from entering your system. There are several types of firewalls, including hardware-based firewalls and software-based firewalls.

Another important cybersecurity tool is antivirus software. Antivirus software helps protect your computer from viruses, malware, and other malicious software. It works by scanning your computer for potential threats and removing them before they can cause damage.

Encryption is also a critical technology for protecting data. Encryption involves converting data into a code that can only be read by authorized users with the correct key. This makes it much more difficult for hackers to access your sensitive information.

Cloud security is another area where cybersecurity tools and technologies are essential. Cloud security involves protecting data stored in the cloud, such as in online storage services like Dropbox or Google Drive. To protect data in the cloud, it's important to use strong passwords, enable two-factor authentication, and encrypt data before uploading it.

Mobile device security is also crucial, as many people now use smartphones and tablets to access sensitive information. Mobile device security tools include antivirus software, firewalls, and encryption, as well as tools that allow you to remotely wipe your device if it's lost or stolen.

Finally, cyber threat intelligence is a critical tool for businesses to stay ahead of potential cyber attacks. This involves monitoring and analyzing threats in real-time, and using this information to develop strategies to prevent attacks before they happen.

In conclusion, there are a wide range of cybersecurity tools and technologies available to help protect your data and systems. By understanding these tools and technologies, businesses and individuals can stay ahead of potential cyber threats and ensure their data remains safe and secure.

Chapter 3: Network Security

What is Network Security?

What is Network Security?

Network security refers to the practice of securing a computer network from unauthorized access, misuse, modification, or denial of service attacks. It is an essential component of any comprehensive digital security strategy, and it is crucial in protecting sensitive information and intellectual property from being compromised.

Network security involves a combination of hardware and software technologies that work together to provide a secure environment for the exchange of information between devices. These technologies include firewalls, intrusion detection and prevention systems (IDPS), virtual private networks (VPNs), secure sockets layer (SSL) certificates, and encryption protocols.

A firewall is a network security device that monitors and controls incoming and outgoing network traffic. It acts as a barrier between the internal network and external networks, such as the Internet, to prevent unauthorized access to the network. Firewalls can also be configured to block specific types of traffic, such as email attachments or file transfers.

IDPS are designed to detect and prevent malicious network activity, such as hacking attempts, malware infections, and denial-of-service attacks. They use various techniques, such as signature-based detection and anomaly detection, to identify threats and take action to mitigate them.

VPNs provide a secure connection between two or more devices over the Internet. They use encryption to protect the data being transmitted, and they can be used to connect remote workers to the internal network or to connect multiple offices in different locations.

SSL certificates are used to secure website traffic by encrypting the data being transmitted between the web server and the user's browser. They provide a way to verify the authenticity of the website and protect against man-in-the-middle attacks.

Encryption protocols, such as Advanced Encryption Standard (AES) and Secure Hash Algorithm (SHA), are used to protect data at rest and in transit. They ensure that sensitive information is unreadable to anyone who does not have the proper decryption key.

In summary, network security is a critical component of any digital security strategy. It involves a combination of hardware and software technologies that work together to protect against unauthorized access, malware infections, and other threats. By implementing effective network security measures, businesses can safeguard their sensitive information and intellectual property from being compromised.

Types of Network Security Threats

In today's digital landscape, businesses and individuals are constantly under threat from various network security threats. These threats come in different forms and can cause significant damage to networks and data. In this subchapter, we will explore the most common types of network security threats that businesses and individuals face.

Malware: Malware is any software designed to harm a computer system or network. It includes viruses, worms, trojan horses, ransomware, and spyware. Malware can enter a system through email attachments, software downloads, or infected websites. Once it infects a system, it can steal data, corrupt files, and cause system crashes.

Phishing: Phishing is a type of social engineering attack that tricks users into revealing sensitive information. It usually comes in the form of an email or website that looks legitimate but is actually a fake. Phishing attacks can steal login credentials, credit card information, and other sensitive data.

Denial-of-Service (DoS) attacks: A DoS attack is an attempt to overwhelm a network or server with traffic to make it unavailable to users. Attackers use botnets or zombie networks to flood a network with traffic until it crashes. DoS attacks can be costly to businesses as they can cause downtime, loss of revenue, and damage to reputation.

Man-in-the-Middle (MitM) attacks: MitM attacks occur when an attacker intercepts communication between two parties. The attacker can then eavesdrop, alter, or steal information. MitM attacks can occur over unsecured Wi-Fi networks, and attackers can use tools like packet sniffers to intercept data.

SQL injection attacks: SQL injection attacks occur when an attacker inserts malicious code into a website's database query. The attacker can then access or modify the database, steal data, or execute commands on the server.

In conclusion, network security threats are a constant threat to businesses and individuals. It is crucial to implement robust security measures to protect against these threats. This includes using antivirus software, firewalls, and encryption tools, as well as training employees on how to detect and avoid phishing attacks. By taking these measures, businesses and individuals can safeguard their data and systems from network security threats.

Network Security Best Practices

In today's world, as technology continues to evolve and businesses become increasingly digital, the need for network security cannot be overstated. With the increasing number of cyber threats and the ever-present risk of data breaches, it is essential to implement best practices for network security to protect your organization's sensitive information.

One of the most critical steps in network security is ensuring that all devices and software are up to date with the latest security patches and updates. These updates often contain critical security fixes that can prevent hackers from exploiting vulnerabilities in your system. It is also crucial to use strong passwords and implement two-factor authentication wherever possible to prevent unauthorized access to your network.

Another best practice for network security is to implement a robust firewall. A firewall acts as a barrier between your network and the internet, blocking unauthorized access to your system while allowing legitimate traffic to pass through. It is also essential to establish strict access controls and limit the number of individuals who have access to your network.

In addition to these measures, it is also important to conduct regular security audits and vulnerability assessments to identify potential weaknesses in your network. These assessments can help you identify areas where security measures can be strengthened, such as implementing more robust encryption protocols or improving your incident response plan.

Finally, it is crucial to have a comprehensive data backup and recovery plan in place. In the event of a cyber attack or data breach, having a backup of your critical data can mean the difference between recovering quickly and experiencing significant downtime and lost revenue.

In conclusion, network security is an essential aspect of any organization's digital security strategy. By implementing the best practices outlined above, you can help protect your organization's sensitive information from cyber threats and ensure the future success of your business.

Network Security Tools and Technologies

Network Security Tools and Technologies

In today's digital age, network security has become a growing concern for businesses of all sizes. With the increasing number of cyber threats, it's essential to have strong network security measures in place to protect your business from potential attacks. This subchapter will delve into some of the network security tools and technologies that can help you safeguard your business.

Firewalls

A firewall is a network security tool that monitors and controls incoming and outgoing network traffic based on predetermined security rules. A firewall acts as a barrier between your internal network and the internet, preventing unauthorized access to your network. Firewalls can be hardware or software-based, and they can be configured to block traffic based on IP addresses, ports, or protocols.

Intrusion Detection Systems (IDS)

An Intrusion Detection System (IDS) is a network security tool that monitors network traffic for signs of suspicious activity. IDSs can detect and alert IT administrators of potential security breaches, such as unauthorized access attempts, malware infections, and network scanning. IDSs can be configured to send alerts to IT administrators via email or SMS, allowing them to respond quickly and prevent a potential cyber attack.

Virtual Private Networks (VPNs)

A Virtual Private Network (VPN) is a network security tool that enables secure remote access to your internal network. A VPN creates an encrypted tunnel between a remote user's device and your internal network, allowing them to access network resources as if they were on-site. VPNs are beneficial for businesses with remote workers or employees who need to access the network from outside the office.

Network Access Control (NAC)

Network Access Control (NAC) is a network security tool that regulates access to your internal network. NAC solutions ensure that only authorized devices can access your network, preventing unauthorized devices from connecting. NAC solutions can be integrated with other network security tools, such as firewalls and IDSs, to provide a comprehensive security solution.

Conclusion

Data Protection 101: A Beginner's Guide to Digital Security

Network security is crucial for the protection of your business from potential cyber threats. By implementing the network security tools and technologies discussed in this subchapter, you can secure your network and safeguard your business from potential attacks. Stay vigilant and keep your network security up to date to ensure your business remains protected from cyber threats.

Chapter 4: Cloud Security

What is Cloud Security?

Cloud security refers to the set of policies, technologies, and controls that are put in place to ensure the protection of data, applications, and infrastructure that are hosted on the cloud. With the rise of cloud computing, businesses are increasingly relying on cloud-based services for their data storage, processing, and computing needs. However, this has also brought about new security risks and challenges. As more and more business-critical data is moved to the cloud, the need for robust cloud security has become paramount.

One of the key challenges of cloud security is the shared responsibility model. While cloud service providers are responsible for the security of the cloud infrastructure, customers are responsible for securing their own applications, data, and user access. This means that a comprehensive cloud security strategy must involve a shared responsibility model between the customer and the cloud service provider.

Another challenge of cloud security is the dynamic nature of cloud environments. Cloud-based applications and services are highly dynamic, with resources being provisioned and deprovisioned on demand. This can make it difficult to maintain visibility and control over the security of the cloud environment. To overcome this challenge, businesses need to implement automated security controls that can adapt to the dynamic nature of the cloud.

Cloud security also involves data protection and privacy. With the increasing amount of sensitive data being stored on the cloud, businesses need to ensure that their data is protected from unauthorized access, theft, and loss. This involves implementing encryption, access controls, and monitoring solutions to detect and respond to security threats.

In summary, cloud security is an essential component of any digital security strategy. It involves a shared responsibility model between the customer and the cloud service provider, automated security controls, and data protection and privacy measures. By implementing a robust cloud security strategy, businesses can ensure the safety and security of their data, applications, and infrastructure on the cloud.

Types of Cloud Security Threats

In the modern world, businesses are relying more and more on cloud computing. Cloud computing offers businesses the ability to store data and access it from anywhere in the world. However, with this convenience comes the risk of cloud security threats. In this subchapter, we will discuss the different types of cloud security threats that businesses need to be aware of.

1. Data Breaches: One of the most common cloud security threats is a data breach. A data breach is when an unauthorized person gains access to confidential information. This can happen when a hacker gains access to a company's cloud storage system. To prevent data breaches, businesses need to ensure that their cloud storage system is secure and that only authorized personnel have access to it.

2. Malware: Malware is software that is designed to harm a computer system. Malware can be installed on a computer system through a variety of means, including email attachments, downloads, and infected websites. Once installed, malware can steal sensitive data and cause other damage to a computer system. To prevent malware from infecting a cloud storage system, businesses need to ensure that their antivirus software is up-to-date and that employees are trained to avoid downloading suspicious files.

3. Denial of Service (DoS) Attacks: A denial of service attack is when an attacker overwhelms a computer system with traffic, making it impossible for legitimate users to access the system. A DoS attack can be launched against a cloud storage system, making it impossible for employees to access their data. To prevent DoS attacks, businesses need to ensure that their cloud storage system can handle a large amount of traffic and that they have a plan in place to mitigate the effects of an attack.

4. Insider Threats: An insider threat is when an employee with access to a company's cloud storage system intentionally or accidentally causes harm to the system. This can include stealing data, deleting data, or introducing malware. To prevent insider threats, businesses need to ensure that employees are properly trained on how to use the cloud storage system and that access to the system is limited to those who need it.

In conclusion, cloud computing offers many benefits to businesses, but it also comes with the risk of cloud security threats. By understanding the different types of threats that exist, businesses can take steps to protect their cloud storage system and ensure that their data is secure.

Cloud Security Best Practices

With the increasing number of cyber attacks targeting cloud infrastructure and the sensitive data hosted on cloud servers, cloud security has become a major concern for businesses of all sizes. In this subchapter, we will discuss some of the best practices for ensuring cloud security and protecting your valuable data.

1. Choose the Right Cloud Provider: The first step in ensuring cloud security is to choose the right cloud provider. Look for a provider with a proven track record of security, compliance, and data protection. Check their certifications and compliance standards to ensure that they meet industry standards.

2. Implement Multi-Factor Authentication: Multi-factor authentication adds an extra layer of security to your cloud account by requiring additional information beyond a password. This can include a security token, fingerprint or facial recognition, or a one-time password sent to your phone or email.

3. Encrypt Your Data: Encryption is an essential tool for protecting your data in the cloud. Use strong encryption algorithms to encrypt your data both in transit and at rest. This will ensure that even if your data is intercepted, it will be useless without the decryption key.

4. Regularly Update Your Software: One of the most common ways hackers gain access to cloud infrastructure is through software vulnerabilities. Regularly updating your software and applying security patches can help prevent these attacks.

5. Use a Virtual Private Network (VPN): A VPN creates a secure, encrypted tunnel between your device and the cloud server, preventing anyone from intercepting your data. It also masks your IP address, making it harder for hackers to track your activity.

6. Monitor Your Cloud Environment: Regularly monitor your cloud environment for any suspicious activity or anomalies. This can include unauthorized access attempts, strange network traffic, or unusual login patterns.

7. Implement Access Controls: Implementing access controls can limit the number of people who have access to your cloud infrastructure. This can include role-based access control, which restricts access based on job responsibilities, or temporary access credentials for contractors or vendors.

By following these best practices, you can ensure that your cloud infrastructure is secure and your data is protected. Remember, cloud security is an ongoing process, so regularly review and update your security practices to stay ahead of the latest threats.

Cloud Security Tools and Technologies

Cloud Security Tools and Technologies

In today's digital age, businesses are moving to the cloud, and with it comes the need for effective cloud security. Cloud security tools and technologies are designed to ensure data protection, privacy, and security in the cloud environment. Cloud security tools include firewalls, intrusion detection systems, encryption, access control, and more.

Firewalls are the first line of defense in cloud security. They filter traffic and prevent unauthorized access to the cloud environment. Intrusion detection systems (IDS) are designed to detect and prevent unauthorized access to the cloud system. They monitor the cloud environment for suspicious activity and alert administrators when a threat is detected.

Encryption is another essential tool in cloud security. It ensures that data is encrypted both in transit and at rest. This means that even if an unauthorized user gains access to the data, they will not be able to read or decipher it. Access control is also critical in cloud security. It ensures that only authorized users have access to the cloud environment and its data.

In addition to these tools, there are also cloud-specific security technologies that businesses can use to ensure data protection. These technologies include cloud access security brokers (CASB), cloud workload protection platforms (CWPP), and cloud security posture management (CSPM).

CASBs are designed to provide visibility and control over cloud applications and data. They help businesses to identify and manage cloud risks, enforce security policies, and ensure compliance. CWPPs provide real-time protection for cloud workloads. They detect and prevent threats to cloud workloads, including malware, intrusions, and data breaches. CSPMs are designed to provide comprehensive security for cloud environments. They help businesses to identify and remediate cloud security risks, ensure compliance, and manage security policies.

Cloud security tools and technologies are essential for businesses that want to protect their data and ensure privacy and security in the cloud environment. With the right tools and technologies, businesses can enjoy the benefits of the cloud without compromising on security.

Chapter 5: Mobile Device Security

What is Mobile Device Security?

Mobile Device Security refers to the measures taken to protect mobile devices, such as smartphones, tablets, and laptops, from cyber threats. With the increasing use of mobile devices for business purposes, ensuring their security has become a critical concern for businesses of all sizes.

Mobile devices have become an integral part of our lives, making it easier to communicate, work, and access information on the go. However, they also present a significant security risk. Mobile devices are vulnerable to a range of cyber threats, such as malware, phishing attacks, and data breaches.

Malware is one of the most common threats to mobile devices. Malware can be installed on a device through a variety of means, such as downloading a malicious app or clicking on a phishing link. Once installed, the malware can steal sensitive information, such as login credentials and financial data.

Phishing attacks are another common threat to mobile devices. These attacks involve tricking users into providing sensitive information, such as login credentials and credit card numbers, by posing as a legitimate entity, such as a bank or social media platform.

Data breaches are also a significant risk for mobile devices. With the increasing amount of sensitive information stored on mobile devices, such as email accounts, social media profiles, and financial data, a data breach can have severe consequences.

To protect mobile devices from these threats, businesses need to implement a range of security measures. These measures include using strong passwords and two-factor authentication, keeping software up to date, using antivirus software, and avoiding risky behaviors, such as downloading apps from untrusted sources.

In conclusion, Mobile Device Security is a critical concern for businesses of all sizes. With the increasing use of mobile devices for business purposes, it is essential to implement robust security measures to protect against cyber threats such as malware, phishing attacks, and data breaches. By taking these measures, businesses can ensure the security of their mobile devices and protect themselves from the potentially devastating consequences of a cyber attack.

Types of Mobile Device Security Threats

Mobile devices have become an integral part of our daily lives, and they are used for a variety of purposes, including communication, entertainment, and business. However, these devices are vulnerable to security threats, and it is important to understand the different types of mobile device security threats to protect your data and privacy.

1. Malware: Malware is malicious software that is designed to damage or disrupt mobile devices. Malware can be downloaded through malicious websites, phishing emails, or infected apps. Once installed, malware can steal personal information, monitor your activity, and even take control of your device.

2. Phishing: Phishing is a type of social engineering attack that is designed to trick users into giving away their personal information. Phishing attacks can be delivered through email, text messages, or social media platforms. A common tactic used by phishers is to create fake websites that look like legitimate ones to steal login credentials and other sensitive information.

3. Man-in-the-Middle Attacks: Man-in-the-Middle (MITM) attacks occur when an attacker intercepts communication between two parties and can eavesdrop on the conversation or alter the messages being transmitted. MITM attacks can be carried out on public Wi-Fi networks or through malware installed on mobile devices.

4. Unsecured Wi-Fi Networks: Public Wi-Fi networks are often unsecured, which makes them vulnerable to eavesdropping and other attacks. Hackers can intercept data transmitted over these networks and steal sensitive information.

5. Physical Theft: Physical theft of mobile devices is also a security threat. If a device is stolen, the thief can access personal information, including contacts, emails, and other sensitive data.

In conclusion, mobile device security threats are a serious concern for individuals and businesses alike. Understanding the different types of threats and taking steps to protect your devices can go a long way in safeguarding your data and privacy. Some best practices to follow include using strong passwords, keeping software up-to-date, avoiding unsecured Wi-Fi networks, and installing anti-virus software.

Mobile Device Security Best Practices

Mobile Device Security Best Practices

In today's digital age, mobile devices have become an integral part of our lives. We use them for communication, entertainment, work, and even banking. However, with this increased dependency on mobile devices, the risk of cyber-attacks has also increased. The good news is that there are several best practices that can be implemented to secure your mobile devices.

1. Keep Your Device up to Date

One of the most important things you can do to protect your mobile device is to keep it updated with the latest software and security patches. Updates often include security fixes that can prevent hackers from exploiting vulnerabilities in your device.

2. Use Strong Passwords or Biometric Authentication

Using strong passwords or biometric authentication (such as fingerprint or facial recognition) is another essential best practice for mobile device security. Avoid using easy-to-guess passwords like "1234" or "password." Instead, use complex passwords that are difficult for anyone to guess.

3. Use Secure Wi-Fi Networks

When using Wi-Fi networks, it is important to ensure that you are connecting to secure networks. Avoid connecting to public Wi-Fi networks that are not password-protected or have weak passwords. Hackers can easily intercept information transmitted over unsecured Wi-Fi networks.

4. Be Wary of Phishing Scams

Phishing scams are common on mobile devices. These scams involve hackers sending fraudulent emails or text messages that appear to be from legitimate sources. They often trick users into giving away their personal information. Be wary of any emails or text messages that request personal information, and avoid clicking links in messages from unknown sources.

5. Use Mobile Device Management (MDM) Solutions

MDM solutions are specifically designed to manage and secure mobile devices. These solutions provide features such as remote wiping, anti-malware protection, and device tracking. They can also ensure that all devices are up to date with the latest software and security patches.

Conclusion

Mobile device security is essential in today's digital age. By following these best practices, you can significantly reduce the risk of cyber-attacks on your mobile devices. Always keep your device up to date, use strong passwords or biometric authentication, use secure Wi-Fi networks, be wary of phishing scams, and use mobile device management solutions. By doing so, you can ensure that your personal and business information remains safe and secure.

Mobile Device Security Tools and Technologies

Data security is an essential element in today's business operations. With the increasing use of mobile devices, the need for mobile device security tools and technologies has become critical. Mobile devices are now ubiquitous in the business world, and they are used to access sensitive data, make transactions, and communicate with colleagues and clients. The use of mobile devices has brought immense convenience, but it has also created new security challenges. To address these challenges, cybersecurity professionals have developed a range of mobile device security tools and technologies.

One of the most important mobile device security tools is mobile device management (MDM) software. MDM software allows organizations to manage and secure their mobile devices from a central location. MDM software can be used to enforce security policies, control access to data, and remotely wipe a device if it is lost or stolen. MDM software is an essential tool for any organization that wants to ensure that its mobile devices are secure and compliant.

Another important mobile device security tool is mobile threat defense (MTD) software. MTD software is designed to protect mobile devices from a wide range of threats, including malware, phishing, and other attacks. MTD software uses machine learning and other advanced techniques to detect and block threats in real-time, ensuring that mobile devices are protected from the latest threats.

Mobile application management (MAM) software is another important mobile device security tool. MAM software allows organizations to manage and secure the applications that are installed on their mobile devices. MAM software can be used to enforce security policies, control access to sensitive data, and block malicious applications. MAM software is an essential tool for any organization that wants to ensure that its mobile applications are secure and compliant.

In addition to these tools, there are also a range of mobile device security technologies that can be used to protect mobile devices. These include biometric authentication, encryption, and secure boot. Biometric authentication can be used to ensure that only authorized users can access a mobile device. Encryption can be used to protect the data that is stored on a mobile device, ensuring that it cannot be accessed by unauthorized users. Secure boot ensures that a mobile device starts up in a secure and trusted environment, preventing attacks that target the boot process.

In conclusion, mobile device security tools and technologies are essential for any organization that wants to ensure the security of its mobile devices and the data that they access. With the increasing use of mobile devices, the need for mobile device security has become critical. By using mobile device management, mobile threat defense, mobile application management, and other security tools and technologies, organizations can ensure that their mobile devices are secure and compliant, protecting their sensitive data and preventing cyberattacks.

Chapter 6: Data Privacy and Protection

What is Data Privacy?

In today's digital age, data privacy has become a crucial topic for individuals and businesses alike. Data privacy refers to the protection of an individual's personal information and the control they have over its collection, storage, and use.

With the rise of technology and the internet, data has become a valuable commodity. Companies collect data from their customers through various means, including online forms, cookies, and social media platforms. However, this collection of data raises concerns about privacy, as individuals may not be aware of how their information is being used or shared.

Data privacy is essential because it helps protect individuals from identity theft, fraud, and other cybercrimes. It also ensures that companies are using individuals' information appropriately and ethically.

Privacy laws, such as the General Data Protection Regulation (GDPR) and the California Consumer Privacy Act (CCPA), have been implemented to regulate the collection, storage, and use of personal data. These laws require companies to obtain individuals' consent before collecting their data and give individuals the right to access, correct, and delete their data.

Data privacy is not only important for individuals but also for businesses. A data breach can result in the loss of customer trust, damage to a company's reputation, and legal and financial consequences. Therefore, implementing strong data privacy and protection measures is essential for businesses to maintain their customers' trust and protect their data from cyber threats.

In conclusion, data privacy refers to the protection of an individual's personal information and the control they have over its collection, storage, and use. It is crucial for individuals and businesses to understand and implement data privacy and protection measures to prevent cyber threats and maintain trust in the digital age.

Why is Data Privacy Important?

Data privacy is a critical aspect of digital security that must not be overlooked by anyone who values their personal or business information. In today's world, where cyber threats and data breaches are rampant, data privacy has become a crucial issue that must be addressed urgently.

Firstly, data privacy is essential because it protects individuals' personal information from malicious actors. Cybercriminals are always on the lookout for valuable data to exploit for their selfish gains. They use various methods, such as phishing, hacking, and malware attacks, to gain access to sensitive information, such as credit card details, social security numbers, and other personal identifiable information. Therefore, ensuring that personal information is kept private and secure is vital in safeguarding individuals' identity and financial well-being.

Secondly, data privacy is crucial for businesses because it helps them maintain their reputation and credibility. In the event of a data breach, businesses risk losing customer trust, which can lead to a loss of revenue and market share. Data breaches can also have legal and regulatory consequences, leading to fines, lawsuits, and even business closure. Therefore, businesses must prioritize data privacy and take proactive measures to ensure that customer information is secure.

Thirdly, data privacy is essential for compliance with data protection regulations. Governments worldwide have enacted laws to protect citizens' personal information from misuse, such as the General Data Protection Regulation (GDPR) in the European Union and the California Consumer Privacy Act (CCPA) in the United States. Failure to comply with these regulations can lead to severe consequences, such as hefty fines and legal actions.

In conclusion, data privacy is an essential aspect of digital security that must not be ignored. It protects individuals' personal information, helps businesses maintain their reputation and credibility, and ensures compliance with data protection regulations. Therefore, individuals and businesses must take proactive measures to safeguard their data and prioritize data privacy in all their digital endeavors.

Data Protection Regulations

Data Protection Regulations

As technology continues to advance and more sensitive information is being digitized, data protection has become a major concern for businesses and individuals alike. Governments around the world have recognized the importance of data protection and have implemented various regulations to safeguard personal and sensitive data. In this chapter, we will explore some of the major data protection regulations that businesses need to be aware of.

General Data Protection Regulation (GDPR)

The GDPR is a European Union regulation that came into effect in May 2018, replacing the 1995 Data Protection Directive. It applies to all companies that process personal data of individuals in the EU, regardless of where the company is located. The regulation aims to give individuals more control over their personal data and requires companies to obtain explicit consent from individuals before collecting and processing their data. Companies must also provide individuals with access to their data and the right to have it deleted. Failure to comply with the GDPR can result in severe penalties, including fines of up to 4% of annual global revenue or €20 million, whichever is greater.

California Consumer Privacy Act (CCPA)

The CCPA is a state-level privacy law that came into effect in January 2020. It applies to companies that collect personal data of California residents and have an annual revenue of more than $25 million, or that collect data from more than 50,000 California residents, or that derive at least 50% of their revenue from selling California residents' personal data. The CCPA gives California residents the right to know what personal data companies are collecting about them, the right to have that data deleted, and the right to opt-out of the sale of their data. Companies that fail to comply with the CCPA can face fines of up to $7,500 per violation.

Cybersecurity Information Sharing Act (CISA)

The CISA is a federal law that was signed into law in 2015. It encourages the sharing of cybersecurity threat information between the government and private sector organizations. The law provides liability protection for companies that voluntarily share cybersecurity information with the government or other companies. The aim of CISA is to improve cybersecurity across all sectors and protect critical infrastructure from cyber attacks.

Conclusion

Data Protection 101: A Beginner's Guide to Digital Security

Data protection regulations are constantly evolving, and it is important for businesses to stay up-to-date with the latest developments. Failure to comply with these regulations can result in severe penalties, damage to business reputation, and loss of customer trust. By implementing robust data protection measures and adhering to relevant regulations, businesses can safeguard their data and protect themselves from cyber threats.

Data Privacy Best Practices

Data Privacy Best Practices

In today's digital age, data privacy is more important than ever before. With the rise of cyber threats, it's essential for businesses to prioritize data privacy best practices to protect their sensitive information and their customers' data.

Here are some best practices for data privacy:

1. Implement strong security measures

Implementing strong security measures is the first step in protecting your data. You should use encryption, firewalls, and anti-virus software to keep your data secure. Make sure you keep all software and systems updated to ensure maximum security.

2. Limit access to data

Limiting access to data is another important best practice for data privacy. Only those who need access to sensitive data should be allowed to access it. You should also use strong passwords and two-factor authentication to ensure that only authorized personnel can access the data.

3. Train your employees

Your employees play a critical role in data privacy. Make sure you train them on best practices for data privacy and security. Teach them how to identify phishing scams and how to handle sensitive information. Regular training sessions can help keep your employees up-to-date on the latest threats and best practices.

4. Have a data breach response plan

Despite your best efforts, data breaches can still occur. Having a data breach response plan in place can help minimize the damage and ensure a quick response. This plan should include steps for mitigating the impact of a breach, notifying customers and authorities, and restoring the system to normal operation.

5. Follow privacy regulations

There are numerous privacy regulations in place that businesses must follow. These regulations vary depending on the industry and location, but they all aim to protect individuals' rights to privacy. Make sure you understand the regulations that apply to your business and take steps to comply with them.

In conclusion, data privacy is a critical component of digital security. By implementing these best practices, businesses can better protect their sensitive information and their customers' data.

Chapter 7: Cyber Threat Intelligence

What is Cyber Threat Intelligence?

In today's digital age, cyber threats have become a critical concern for businesses and organizations worldwide. As the number of cyber attacks continues to rise, it is essential to have an effective cybersecurity strategy in place to protect sensitive data and prevent potential breaches. One crucial aspect of this strategy is Cyber Threat Intelligence (CTI).

CTI can be defined as the knowledge and insights gained from analyzing data about potential cyber threats and attacks. This information helps organizations to identify and mitigate potential risks, and to stay one step ahead of cybercriminals. CTI includes a wide range of data sources, such as malware analysis, threat actor behavior, vulnerability intelligence, and social media monitoring.

To effectively use CTI, organizations need to have a comprehensive understanding of their own cybersecurity posture, as well as the threat landscape. This involves not only understanding the technical aspects of cyber threats but also the motivations behind them. For example, while some cyber attacks are financially motivated, others are politically motivated or carried out by hacktivists.

CTI can be used to inform a range of cybersecurity decisions, from developing incident response plans to prioritizing security investments. By providing real-time and up-to-date information about potential threats, CTI can help organizations to take a proactive approach to cybersecurity, rather than simply reacting to incidents as they occur.

One challenge with CTI, however, is that the threat landscape is constantly evolving, and cybercriminals are constantly finding new ways to attack. This means that organizations need to continually update their CTI sources and strategies to stay ahead of the curve.

Overall, Cyber Threat Intelligence is a critical component of any effective cybersecurity strategy. By providing organizations with a deeper understanding of potential threats and how to mitigate them, CTI can help to prevent data breaches and minimize the impact of cyber attacks on businesses and their customers.

Types of Cyber Threat Intelligence

Cyber Threat Intelligence (CTI) is the process of gathering, analyzing, and disseminating information about potential cyber threats. It is an essential aspect of cybersecurity, as it allows organizations to stay ahead of potential attacks and respond quickly to any incidents that may occur. There are many different types of CTI, each with its own strengths and weaknesses.

The first type of CTI is technical intelligence. This involves the collection and analysis of data from various technical sources, such as network logs, malware samples, and vulnerability reports. Technical intelligence is useful for identifying specific threats and vulnerabilities, as well as for developing effective mitigation strategies.

The second type of CTI is operational intelligence. This involves the collection and analysis of data about the activities of cybercriminals and other threat actors. Operational intelligence is useful for understanding the tactics, techniques, and procedures used by these actors, as well as for identifying potential targets and vulnerabilities.

The third type of CTI is strategic intelligence. This involves the collection and analysis of data about the broader threat landscape, including emerging trends, threat actors, and geopolitical factors. Strategic intelligence is useful for understanding the larger context in which cyber threats operate, as well as for developing long-term security strategies.

Another important type of CTI is tactical intelligence. This involves the collection and analysis of data about specific incidents or attacks, with the goal of identifying the attackers, their motivations, and their capabilities. Tactical intelligence is useful for responding quickly to specific incidents and for developing targeted mitigation strategies.

Finally, there is also human intelligence, which involves the collection and analysis of data from human sources, such as insiders or other sources of information. Human intelligence is useful for identifying potential threats that may not be apparent from technical or operational data alone, as well as for providing context and insight into the motivations and tactics of threat actors.

In conclusion, there are many different types of CTI, each with its own strengths and weaknesses. Organizations must carefully consider their specific needs and goals when selecting and implementing a CTI program, and must also ensure that they have the necessary resources and expertise to effectively gather, analyze, and disseminate intelligence about potential cyber threats. With the right approach to CTI, organizations can stay ahead of potential attacks and protect their digital assets from harm.

Data Protection 101: A Beginner's Guide to Digital Security

Cyber Threat Intelligence Best Practices

Cyber Threat Intelligence Best Practices

In today's digital landscape, cyber threats are becoming more sophisticated and frequent, making it more challenging for businesses to protect themselves. Cyber Threat Intelligence (CTI) is essential for organizations to stay ahead of potential threats and quickly respond to any incidents that occur.

Here are some best practices for implementing an effective CTI program:

1. Understand your organization's needs: Before implementing a CTI program, it's crucial to understand your organization's unique needs. This includes identifying critical assets, assessing potential threats, and understanding the level of risk tolerance.

2. Establish a CTI team: Building a dedicated CTI team is essential for gathering and analyzing threat intelligence. The team should consist of individuals with a variety of skill sets, including threat analysts, security researchers, and data scientists.

3. Collect and analyze data: Gathering and analyzing data is a critical component of CTI. This includes collecting data from internal and external sources, such as social media and dark web forums. The data should be analyzed to identify patterns and potential threats.

4. Share intelligence: CTI is only effective if it's shared with the relevant stakeholders. This includes sharing intelligence with the security team, executives, and external partners. Sharing intelligence can help prevent future attacks and reduce the impact of any incidents that occur.

5. Stay up-to-date: Cyber threats are constantly evolving, so it's essential to stay up-to-date with the latest trends and best practices. This includes attending industry conferences, participating in information-sharing communities, and staying informed about new threats and vulnerabilities.

Data Protection 101: A Beginner's Guide to Digital Security

Implementing an effective CTI program can be time-consuming and complex, but it's essential for protecting your organization from cyber threats. By following these best practices, you can establish a robust CTI program that helps you stay ahead of potential threats and respond quickly to any incidents that occur.

Cyber Threat Intelligence Tools and Technologies

Cyber threat intelligence is an essential aspect of cybersecurity. Threat intelligence provides insight into the tactics, techniques, and procedures (TTPs) that attackers use when attempting to exploit vulnerabilities in your network or applications. Cyber threat intelligence tools and technologies are instrumental in gathering and analyzing this data, allowing organizations to identify potential threats and take proactive measures to mitigate them.

One of the most critical cyber threat intelligence tools is a Security Information and Event Management (SIEM) system. A SIEM system collects and analyzes log data from various sources, including network devices, firewalls, servers, and applications, to identify potential threats. The system uses machine learning algorithms to identify anomalies and trends in the data, enabling security teams to take prompt action when a threat is detected.

Another essential tool in the cyber threat intelligence arsenal is the intrusion detection system (IDS). An IDS is a software application that monitors network traffic for suspicious activity, including unauthorized access attempts, malware infections, and other security threats. When the system detects a potentially harmful event, it generates an alert that is sent to the security team for further investigation and response.

Advanced threat intelligence platforms (ATIPs) are another critical component of a comprehensive cyber threat intelligence strategy. These platforms use machine learning algorithms and artificial intelligence (AI) to analyze vast amounts of data from multiple sources, including social media, dark web forums, and other online sources. ATIPs can identify emerging threats, assess their potential impact, and provide recommendations for mitigating their effects.

Finally, threat intelligence feeds are an essential tool for organizations seeking to stay ahead of the latest threats. These feeds provide real-time updates on emerging threats, including malware, phishing, and other types of attacks. Organizations can use this information to adjust their security policies and procedures, apply patches and updates, and take other proactive measures to protect their networks and data.

In conclusion, cyber threat intelligence tools and technologies are essential for organizations seeking to protect their networks, applications, and data from the ever-evolving threat landscape. These tools enable security teams to identify potential threats, take prompt action to mitigate them, and stay ahead of emerging threats in real-time. By leveraging these tools, organizations can improve their cybersecurity posture and reduce the risk of costly data breaches and other security incidents.

Chapter 8: Future of Data Protection

Emerging Technologies in Data Protection

Emerging Technologies in Data Protection

As technology continues to advance, so does the need for data protection. With the rise of cyber threats, businesses need to invest in innovative technologies that can secure their sensitive information. Here are some emerging technologies in data protection that can help keep your data safe.

1. Blockchain

Blockchain technology is a decentralized database that stores information across a network of computers. It is highly secure because it uses cryptographic algorithms to ensure that no one can tamper with the data. Blockchain can be used for different applications such as financial transactions, supply chain management, and identity verification.

2. Artificial Intelligence

Artificial Intelligence (AI) can be used to automate data protection processes such as threat detection and response. AI algorithms can analyze large amounts of data and identify patterns that could indicate a cyber attack. AI can also be used to monitor user behavior and detect anomalies that could signal a security breach.

3. Quantum Computing

Quantum computing is a new technology that uses quantum mechanics to process information. It has the potential to revolutionize data protection because it can perform complex calculations that are impossible for traditional computers. Quantum computing can be used to crack encryption codes, which means that new encryption methods will need to be developed to keep data secure.

4. Homomorphic Encryption

Homomorphic encryption is a form of encryption that allows data to be processed without being decrypted. This means that sensitive data can be processed securely without ever being exposed. Homomorphic encryption can be used for applications such as cloud computing and data analytics.

5. Edge Computing

Edge computing is a distributed computing model that brings computation and data storage closer to the devices that need it. This reduces the amount of data that needs to be transmitted over the network, which can improve security. Edge computing can also be used to process sensitive data locally, which reduces the risk of data breaches.

In conclusion, emerging technologies in data protection are essential for businesses that want to keep their data safe. Blockchain, AI, quantum computing, homomorphic encryption, and edge computing are just a few examples of the innovative technologies that can help secure sensitive information. As technology continues to evolve, so does the need for new and innovative data protection solutions.

Predictions for the Future of Data Protection

As technology continues to advance and our dependence on digital devices and online services grows, the importance of data protection cannot be overstated. With the proliferation of cyber attacks, data breaches, and privacy violations, it is clear that the future of data protection is becoming increasingly complex and challenging.

One prediction for the future of data protection is that there will be a greater emphasis on privacy and data sovereignty. With the introduction of new laws and regulations such as the EU's General Data Protection Regulation (GDPR) and the California Consumer Privacy Act (CCPA), companies will be required to take a more proactive approach to protecting their customers' data. This will involve implementing stronger security measures, conducting regular audits and risk assessments, and providing greater transparency around how data is collected, used, and shared.

Another key trend in the future of data protection is the increasing use of artificial intelligence (AI) and machine learning (ML) to detect and respond to cyber threats. As cyber attacks become more sophisticated and complex, traditional security measures such as firewalls and antivirus software will no longer be sufficient. AI and ML will enable organizations to better identify and respond to threats in real-time, providing a more proactive approach to cyber security.

Cloud security will also be an important area of focus in the future of data protection. With the majority of businesses now using cloud-based services, securing the cloud has become a critical priority. This will involve implementing stronger encryption and access controls, as well as conducting regular vulnerability assessments and penetration testing.

Mobile device security will also be a key area of concern in the future of data protection. As more people use their mobile devices for work and personal use, the risk of data breaches and cyber attacks increases. This will require companies to implement stronger security measures such as multi-factor authentication, device encryption, and remote wipe capabilities.

Finally, the future of data protection will require a more collaborative approach between businesses, governments, and consumers. Cybersecurity threats are a global issue that require a coordinated response. This will involve sharing threat intelligence, collaborating on best practices, and providing greater education and awareness around the importance of data protection.

In conclusion, the future of data protection will be characterized by greater complexity, sophistication, and collaboration. While the challenges may be great, the opportunities for innovation and progress are equally significant. By staying ahead of the curve and investing in the latest security technologies and practices, businesses can protect their customers' data and ensure a secure, digital future for all.

Conclusion

In conclusion, data protection is crucial in today's digital world. As technology continues to advance, the risks of cyber threats and attacks also increase. Therefore, it is essential for individuals and businesses to implement strong security measures to protect their sensitive information.

Cybersecurity, network security, cloud security, mobile device security, data privacy and protection, and cyber threat intelligence are all important aspects of data protection. Each of these areas plays a vital role in safeguarding data against various threats and vulnerabilities.

As a trade audience interested in technology and business, it is important to stay updated with the latest trends and developments in data protection. Learning about new security measures, best practices, and emerging threats can help you stay ahead of the game and protect your data more effectively.

Data Protection 101: A Beginner's Guide to Digital Security

Moreover, companies that prioritize data protection not only protect their sensitive information, but they also gain the trust of their customers. Customers are more likely to do business with companies that prioritize their privacy and security.

In summary, data protection is a critical aspect of digital security. It is essential for individuals and businesses to take proactive measures to safeguard their sensitive information. By implementing strong security measures and staying informed about emerging threats, we can all contribute to a safer and more secure digital world.

Appendix: Data Protection Resources

Data Protection Organizations

Data Protection Organizations

In today's digital age, data protection is more important than ever before. With the rise of cyber threats and data breaches, organizations must take the necessary steps to protect their sensitive data and ensure the privacy of their customers. To achieve this, many organizations turn to data protection organizations for guidance and support.

Data protection organizations are non-profit entities that provide resources and guidance to organizations on how to protect their data. These organizations play a vital role in ensuring that businesses are equipped with the necessary tools and knowledge to defend against cyber threats.

One such organization is the International Association of Privacy Professionals (IAPP). The IAPP is the largest and most comprehensive global information privacy community. It provides resources and support to over 50,000 members worldwide, including professionals in the fields of privacy, data protection, and cybersecurity.

Another prominent data protection organization is the National Cyber Security Alliance (NCSA). The NCSA is a non-profit organization that works to raise awareness about cybersecurity and provide resources and tools to individuals and organizations to help them stay safe online.

In addition to these organizations, there are several others that provide valuable resources and support to organizations seeking to improve their data protection efforts. These organizations include the Cloud Security Alliance, the Information Systems Security Association, and the Cyber Threat Alliance.

By partnering with these data protection organizations, businesses can gain access to a wealth of knowledge and resources that can help them improve their cybersecurity posture. From training and certification programs to best practices and industry insights, these organizations can provide the support and guidance that businesses need to stay ahead of the ever-evolving threat landscape.

In conclusion, data protection organizations play a critical role in helping businesses protect their sensitive data and ensure the privacy of their customers. By partnering with these organizations, businesses can gain access to the knowledge and resources they need to defend against cyber threats and stay ahead of the curve in the ever-changing world of digital security.

Data Protection Tools and Technologies

Data Protection Tools and Technologies

As the world becomes increasingly digitized, the need for robust data protection tools and technologies has never been more important. Cybersecurity, network security, cloud security, mobile device security, data privacy and protection and cyber threat intelligence are all areas that require our attention in order to safeguard our digital assets.

One of the most important data protection tools is encryption. Encryption is the process of converting plain text into coded text which can only be deciphered with a key. Encryption helps to protect sensitive data from being intercepted and understood by unauthorized parties. There are many encryption tools available, including open-source encryption software like VeraCrypt and GnuPG.

Another important data protection tool is antivirus software. Antivirus software monitors for and detects malicious software or malware, such as viruses, trojans, and worms. Antivirus software can also help to prevent attack vectors such as phishing emails and drive-by downloads. There are many antivirus software options available in the market, including Norton, McAfee, and Kaspersky.

Firewalls are another key data protection tool. A firewall is a network security system that monitors and controls incoming and outgoing network traffic based on predetermined security rules. Firewalls can help to prevent unauthorized access to your systems and data. There are various types of firewalls, including hardware firewalls, software firewalls, and cloud firewalls.

Virtual Private Networks (VPNs) are also important data protection tools. VPNs create a secure and encrypted connection between your device and the internet, allowing you to browse the web anonymously and securely. VPNs can be used to protect your online activity from prying eyes, and to access restricted content or websites. There are many VPN providers available, including NordVPN, ExpressVPN, and Surfshark.

In conclusion, data protection is a critical issue in today's digital world. Choosing the right data protection tools and technologies can help to safeguard your digital assets and ensure that your data remains secure from unauthorized access. By implementing the right tools and technologies, you can protect your business and personal data from cyber threats, and enjoy peace of mind knowing that your digital assets are secure.

Data Protection Regulations and Standards

Data Protection Regulations and Standards

The increasing reliance on technology in business operations has led to the need for more stringent data protection regulations and standards. With the influx of cyber threats targeting sensitive information, data protection has become a critical concern for organizations seeking to keep their operations running smoothly and maintain their reputation.

In this chapter, we will explore the various data protection regulations and standards that businesses need to adhere to. We will also discuss the importance of data privacy and protection and how it relates to cybersecurity, network security, cloud security, mobile device security, and cyber threat intelligence.

Data Protection Regulations

The General Data Protection Regulation (GDPR) is one of the most comprehensive data protection regulations in the world. It came into effect in the European Union (EU) in May 2018 and applies to all organizations that process personal data of EU citizens. The GDPR outlines strict guidelines on how businesses should collect, store, and use personal data. Failure to comply with the GDPR can result in hefty fines of up to €20 million or 4% of the company's global annual revenue, whichever is higher.

Other data protection regulations include the California Consumer Privacy Act (CCPA) and the Health Insurance Portability and Accountability Act (HIPAA), which apply to healthcare organizations that handle sensitive patient information.

Data Protection Standards

Various data protection standards have been developed to help organizations protect their data. The Payment Card Industry Data Security Standard (PCI DSS) outlines the security measures that businesses that accept credit card payments must implement to protect cardholder data. The ISO/IEC 27001 is another data protection standard that provides a framework for managing and securing business information.

Importance of Data Privacy and Protection

Data privacy and protection are critical concerns for organizations as they seek to protect their customers' sensitive information. Failure to protect this data can lead to reputational damage, loss of customer trust, and legal consequences.

Cybersecurity, Network Security, Cloud Security, Mobile Device Security, and Cyber Threat Intelligence

Data protection regulations and standards are closely related to cybersecurity, network security, cloud security, mobile device security, and cyber threat intelligence. These aspects of digital security are essential in ensuring that organizations protect their data from cyber threats.

In conclusion, data protection regulations and standards play a critical role in ensuring that organizations protect their sensitive information from cyber threats. As businesses continue to rely on technology, it is essential to adhere to these regulations and standards to maintain customer trust and safeguard their reputation.